50 More Classic Melodies for Organ

kevin mayhew

**kevin
mayhew**

First published in Great Britain in 1999 by Kevin Mayhew Ltd
Buxhall, Stowmarket, Suffolk IP14 3BW
Tel: +44 (0) 1449 737978 Fax: +44 (0) 1449 737834
E-mail: info@kevinmayhewltd.com

www.kevinmayhew.com

9 8 7 6 5 4 3 2 1 0

ISBN 978 1 84003 306 9
ISMN M 57004 503 7
Catalogue No. 1400202

Cover design: Rob Mortonson
© Images used under licence from Shutterstock Inc.
Proofreading: Helen Goodall

Printed and bound in Great Britain

Contents

FIRST MOVEMENT from 'ITALIAN' SYMPHONY

Felix Mendelssohn (1809-1847) arr. Malcolm McKelvey

Sw.: 8' 4' 2' Mixt.
Gt.: 8' 4' 2'
Ped.: 16' 8'
Sw. to Gt.; Sw. to Ped.

+ Gt. to Ped.

WEDDING DAY AT TROLDHAUGEN

Edvard Grieg (1843-1907) arr. Malcolm McKelvey

Ch.: Soft Reed 8'; Sw.: 16' 8' 4' 2'; Gt.: 8' 4' 2'; Ped.: 16' 8'
Sw. to Gt.; Sw. to Ped.

LARGO AL FACTOTUM from 'THE BARBER OF SEVILLE'

Gioachino Rossini (1792-1868) arr. Quentin Thomas

Sw. to Gt.; Sw. to Ped.; Gt. to Ped.

Poco meno mosso

poco rall.

18

IN THE HALL OF THE MOUNTAIN KING
from 'PEER GYNT'

Edvard Grieg (1843-1907) arr. Adrian Vernon Fish

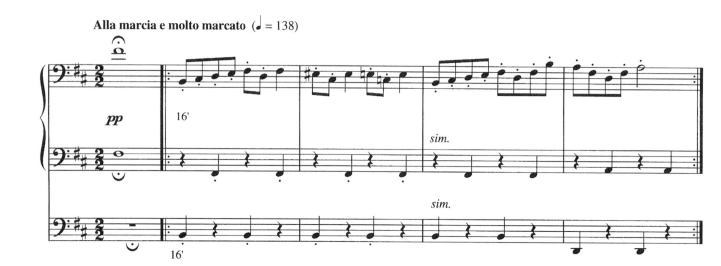

FUNERAL MARCH from 'EROICA' SYMPHONY

Ludwig van Beethoven (1770-1827) arr. Adrian Vernon Fish

FIRST MOVEMENT from CELLO CONCERTO

Antonín Dvorák (1841-1904) arr. Quentin Thomas

Sw. Full – 16's; Gt. Large diap. (no 16's); Ped. No reeds. 16' + 8'
Sw. to Gt.; Sw. to Ped.

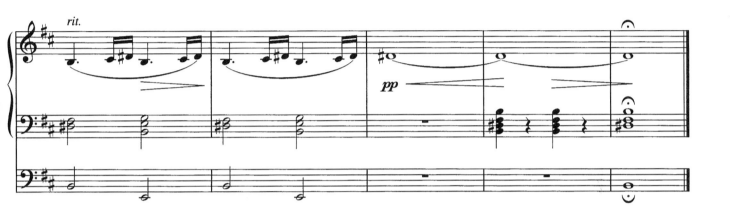

31

FINALE from TRUMPET CONCERTO

Joseph Haydn (1732-1809) arr. Malcolm McKelvey

34

+ Gt. to Ped.

Gt.   Tpt.   Gt.

Gt.   tr

35

SLOW MOVEMENT from
FLUTE AND HARP CONCERTO

Wolfgang Amadeus Mozart (1756-1791) arr. Martin Setchell

41

RIDE OF THE VALKYRIES

Richard Wagner (1813-1883) arr. Andrew Gant

(increase Gt.)

ff

45

OVERTURE to 'DIDO AND AENEAS'

Henry Purcell (1659-1695) arr. Malcolm McKelvey

THEME from 1812 OVERTURE

Peter Ilyich Tchaikovsky (1840-1893) arr. James Patten

URLICHT from SYMPHONY No. 2 'RESURRECTION'

Gustav Mahler (1860-1911) arr. Adrian Vernon Fish

FIRST MOVEMENT from VIOLIN CONCERTO IN A MINO

Johann Sebastian Bach (1685-1750) arr. Malcolm McKelvey

Gt.: 8' 4' 2'; Sw.: 8' 4' Mixt.; Ch.: 8' 2'
Ped.: 16' 8'
Sw. to Gt.

- Gt. to Ped. ***p***

Sw. ***p***

Gt. ***f***

+ Gt. to Ped.

QUARTET from 'RIGOLETTO'

Giuseppe Verdi (1813-1901) arr. Martin Setchell

65

THIRD MOVEMENT from SYMPHONY No. 3

Johannes Brahms (1833-1897) arr. James Patten

MAZURKA from 'COPPÉLIA'

Léo Delibes (1836-1891) arr. Martin Setchell

71

72

Tempo I

MARCH from 'TANNHÄUSER'

Richard Wagner (1813-1883) arr. Richard Lloyd

SECOND MOVEMENT from SYMPHONY NO. 7

Ludwig van Beethoven (1770-1827) arr. James Patten

84

FIRST MOVEMENT from DIVERTIMENTO IN D

Wolfgang Amadeus Mozart (1756-1791) arr. Malcolm McKelvey

Gt.: 8' 4'; Sw.: 8' 4' 2'; Ped.: 16' 8'
Sw. to Ped.

HUNGARIAN RHAPSODY from RÁKÓCZI MARCH

Franz Liszt (1811-1886) arr. Malcolm McKelvey

Un poco meno allegro

dolce

marcato con grazia

Gt. **ff**

95

Full Organ

97

MEDITATION from 'THAÏS'

Jules Massenet (1842-1912) arr. Andrew Moore

ABENDSTERN

Richard Wagner (1813-1883) arr. James Patten

OVERTURE to 'A MIDSUMMER NIGHT'S DREAM'

Felix Mendelssohn (1809-1847) arr. Colin Hand

PIE JESU from 'REQUIEM'

Gabriel Fauré (1845-1924) arr. Martin Setchell

LA TRAVIATA Act 3

Giuseppe Verdi (1813-1901) arr. Richard Lloyd

111

OVERTURE to 'RUSLAN AND LUDMILA'

Mikhail Glinka (1804-1857) arr. Adrian Vernon Fish

SLOW MOVEMENT from 'EMPEROR' CONCERTO

Ludwig van Beethoven (1770-1827) arr. Malcolm McKelvey

Sw.: Salicional
Gt.: Gamba
Ped.: Dulciana 16'
Sw. to Gt.; Sw. to Ped.

117

SIEGFRIED IDYLL

Richard Wagner (1813-1883) arr. Andrew Moore

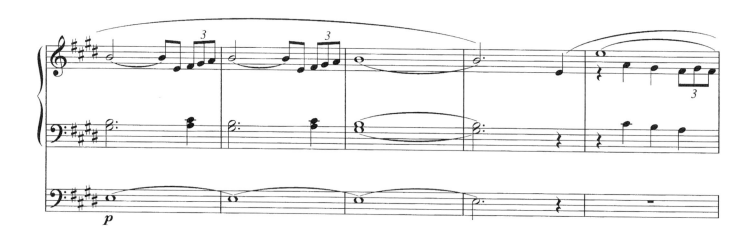

PRÉLUDE À L'APRÈS-MIDI D'UN FAUNE

Claude Debussy (1862-1918) arr. Adrian Vernon Fish

IL MIO TESORO from 'DON GIOVANNI'

Wolfgang Amadeus Mozart (1756-1791) arr. James Patten

SECOND MOVEMENT from PIANO CONCERTO

Edvard Grieg (1843-1907) arr. James Patten

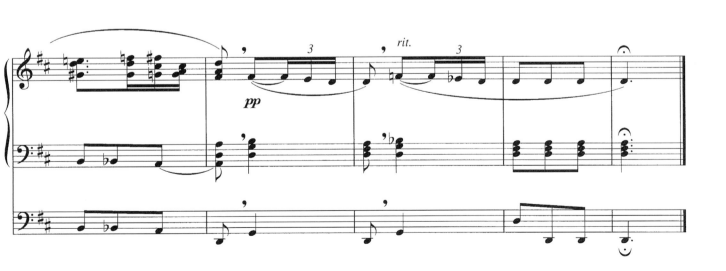

O MIO BABBINO CARO from 'GIANNI SCHICCHI'

Giacomo Puccini (1858-1924) arr. Andrew Gant

FIRST MOVEMENT from PIANO CONCERTO NO. 1

Peter Ilyich Tchaikovsky (1840-1893) arr. Richard Lloyd

PROCESSION OF THE GUESTS from 'TANNHÄUSER'

Richard Wagner (1813-1883) arr. James Patten

ossia ♪ ♪

ossia ♪ ♪

sim.

cresc.

138

139

FOR UNTO US A CHILD IS BORN from 'MESSIAH'

George Frideric Handel (1685-1759) arr. Andrew Gant

144

MARCH TO THE SCAFFOLD
from 'SYMPHONIE FANTASTIQUE'

Hector Berlioz (1803-1869) arr. Adrian Vernon Fish

151

LAST MOVEMENT from VIOLIN CONCERTO No. 1

Nicolò Paganini (1782-1840) arr. Malcolm McKelvey

Sw.: Flute 8' 4'; Gt.: Diapason 8', Principal 4'
Ch.: Viola 8' 4', Piccolo 2'; Ped.: Bourdon 16'
Sw. to Gt.; Sw. to Ped.

BADINERIE from SUITE NO. 2

Johann Sebastian Bach (1685-1750) arr. Richard Lloyd

SECOND MOVEMENT from SYMPHONY No. 5

Peter Ilyich Tchaikovsky (1840-1893) arr. Andrew Moore

FIRST MOVEMENT from
HARPSICHORD CONCERTO IN D MINOR

Johann Sebastian Bach (1685-1750) arr. Adrian Vernon Fish

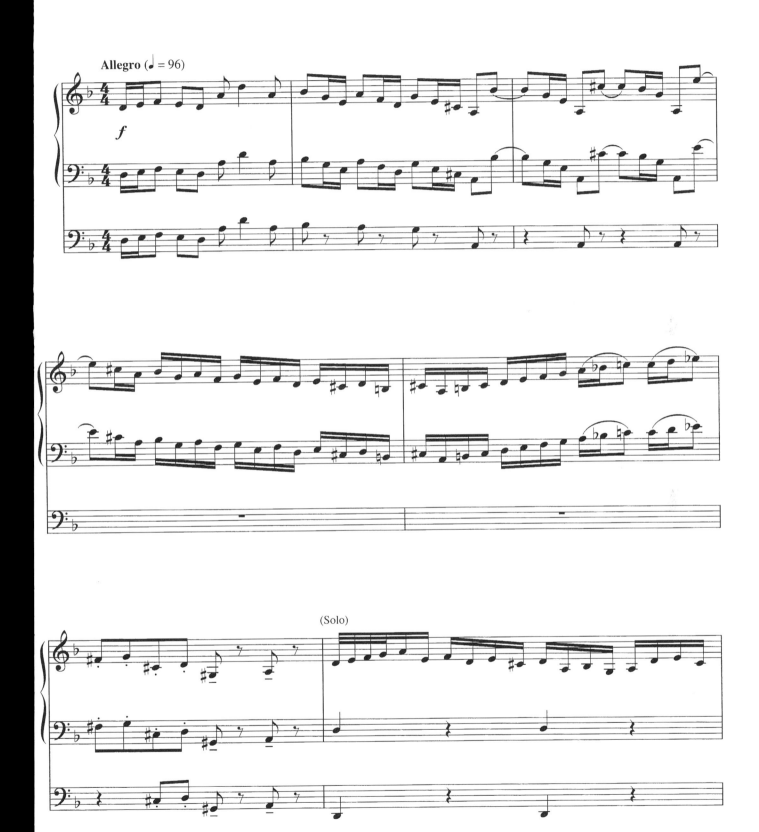

LAUDATE DOMINUM from 'EXULTATE JUBILATE'

Wolfgang Amadeus Mozart (1756-1791) arr. Quentin Thomas

Sw. Stgs. + Fl.
Gt. Solo diap.
Ped. 16'
Sw. to Ped.

DANSE MACABRE

Camille Saint-Saëns (1835-1921) arr. Malcolm McKelvey

Gt.: 8' 4'; Sw.: 8' 4' 2'; Ch.: 8' Dulciana
Ped.: 16' Bourdon, 8' Flute
(No couplers)

173

THEMES from CAPRICCIO ITALIEN

Peter Ilyich Tchaikovsky (1840-1893) arr. Adrian Vernon Fish

176

ST. ANTHONY CHORALE

Joseph Haydn (1732-1809) adapted by Johannes Brahms (1833-1897)
arr. Colin Hand

FIRST MOVEMENT from SYMPHONY No. 40

Wolfgang Amadeus Mozart (1756-1791) arr. Malcolm McKelvey

Sw: 8' 4' Strings
Gt: 8' 4' 2' Diapasons
Ch: 8' 4' Flutes; Nazard 2⅔'
Ped: 16' 8' Flutes
Sw. to Gt.; Sw. to Ped.

- Gt. to Ped.

184

+ Gt. to Ped.

ALLEGRETTO from 'SINFONIETTA'

Leos Janácek (1854-1928) arr. Adrian Vernon Fish

189

CLAIR DE LUNE

Claude Debussy (1862-1918) arr. James Patten

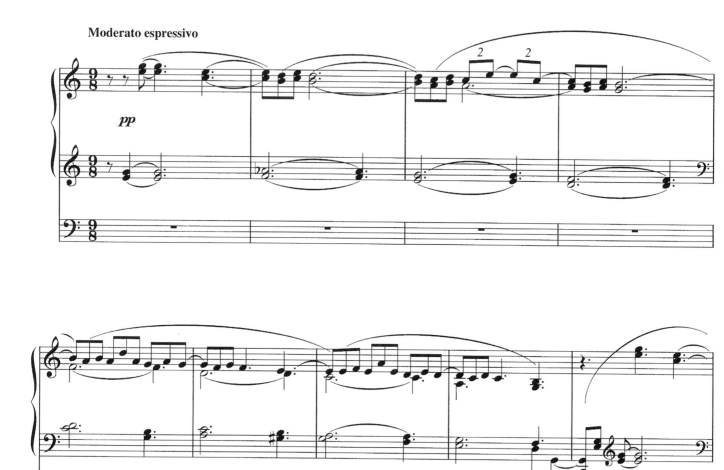

UNA VOCE POCO FA
from 'THE BARBER OF SEVILLE'

Gioachino Rossini (1792-1868) arr. Malcolm McKelvey

Sw.: 8' 4' 2'; Gt.: 16' 8' 4' 2'; Ch.: 8' 4' 2⅔'; Ped.: 16' 8'
Sw. to Gt.; Sw. to Ped.; Gt. to Ped.

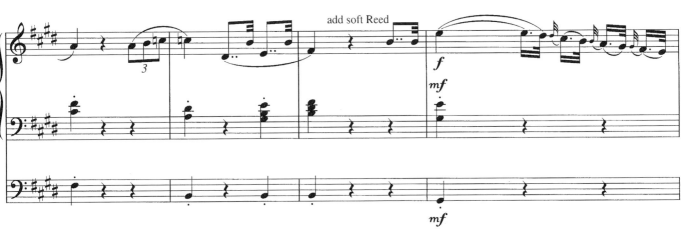

© Copyright 1999 Kevin Mayhew Ltd.
It is illegal to photocopy music.

193

CANTIQUE DE JEAN RACINE

Gabriel Fauré (1845-1924) arr. Martin Setchell

FOURTH MOVEMENT from
SONATA FOR VIOLIN AND PIANO

César Franck (1822-1890) arr. Malcolm McKelvey

Sw.: 8' 4' + Sub-Oct.; Gt.: 16' 8' 2'; Ped.: 16' 8'
Sw. to Gt.; Sw. to Ped.